SEA CHESTS
OR A
CARRY-ON

POEMS BY

BILL NEWBY

Bill.Newby.wordsmith@gmail.com

ISBN-10: 1983535745
ISBN-13: 978-1983535741

for Barbara

ACKNOWLEDGEMENTS

Thanks to the editors of the following
where some of these poems first appeared,
sometimes in slightly different form:

The Bluffton Breeze: The beach was bare tonight
                         Mockingbird DJ

Ohio Teachers Write: Mother's Wish

Time & Tide (Island Writers' Network):
                         Crossing the Blue Ridge Gap
                         ¡Qué Lástima!

Panoplyzine: The Harrow

CONTENTS

Crossing the Blue Ridge Gap

You are There

Sea Chests or a Carry-On

Waiting for an Open Door

CROSSING THE BLUE RIDGE GAP

Sixty

It used to be the posted limit,
the number on the dial
of my '56 Olds
above which I tried to hold the needle
as I drove from Chicago to Cleveland.

An easy task when dry,
except for leg cramps
or slow traffic choking the road.

Much harder in the rain
or a winter snow,
when my wipers couldn't clear the splatter
or the road felt as slick
as the ice we cleaned
at Forest Hills Park
to spend the afternoon
sprinting for the puck.

Cars improved.
Oil got cheaper.
Politicians caved,
and limits were raised.

Now,
merely keeping pace,
I often discover
the eighty on my dash—

an eighty that doesn't
shoot me past others
or prompt the highway patrol

to launch a gravel spitting pursuit,

an eighty that feels
solid and smooth.

In childhood
as we raced across the ice,
elbowing each other for the best line,
then tumbling into the punishing crust
of surrounding snow,

we'd fall laughing
and take pleasure
in our burning cheeks
and trembling legs,
then flip over
for another go.

Our youth seemed eternal
in those winter days,

but we were also hungry
to pack in experience –
to stuff our days with tumble and risk
before our joints stiffened
or we'd have to straighten a tie
and head off for an nine-to-five.

And sixty,
sixty seemed decrepit,
bent over, hobbled,
out-to-pasture frail,
decades beyond our imagination,
continents beyond our reach.

But now,
as sixty approaches,
when the needle is about to eclipse that mark,
eighty seems not far away —

and maybe even
as solid and smooth
as the sixty on the horizon.

And though it takes longer now
to flip over and regain good footing,
there are many more days
to stuff with tumble and risk.

Let it snow.

Tee Time for Ben

We can leave the remote on the shelf
and the recliner empty.

We don't need to see the leaderboard
to know what we've lost.

He was a champion's champion,
whose favorite club was a smile.

In recent interviews about all-star players,
the rough complained,
"No matter how much we schemed
with sand and stream,
he always kept his balance."

And after years of speculation,
the wind finally admitted,
"He often sent me poems
and stroked my cheek.
We had a long affair."

The greens added
that he studied them like a scholar
and stood confident and hopeful
over every putt.

Ben walked the course with love
and filled his scorecard with friends.

And now that he's retired,
there is no doubt:
he'd be displeased

if we didn't celebrate his game,
and if we failed
to stuff his memory in our bag
as we play through.

Mother's Wish

Cast me into the wind
when your fingers can no longer hold me.

Do not grieve
but raise a smile,
a glass,
a neighbor's hand,
and celebrate my joy.

Cast me to the wind,
and let the earth
spin my memory
into your heart.

No ground should swallow.
No preacher postulate.

Set me free
in open air, clear sky, and fresh cut fairways.

Set me free
and lift your spirit,
look about you,
enjoy the day.
Take comfort in a lover's eye,
a neighbor's laugh,
the smell of barbecue,
the softness of a baby's cheek.

Don't cry.
Don't mourn.

My life was full.

Set me free.
Set me free.
Set me free.

Crossing the Blue Ridge Gap

Heading south, some ten miles out,
the warning signs begin.

Travel Advisory.
Dense Fog Ahead.
Beware of Stopped Vehicles.

It's a long, slow climb
from northern chill to southern ease,
from months of goodbyes
to the uncertainty of new friendships.

We've passed through the gap repeatedly,
anticipating retirement and returning to work,
surveying new neighborhoods and going back home.

The apex has often been clouded with a milky broth
barely stirred by the tail lights ahead –
a fog so thick we've needed to slow our advance
to a squinting, tight-knuckled caution.

But yesterday we watched
as the moving van swallowed all our stuff,
and today we crossed the gap
under a crystal clear nightfall.

And as we coasted down the southeastern face,
the valley below and the countryside beyond
shimmered like diamonds
cast across pillows of black velvet,
and the road ahead felt dry and firm.

Cialis "Expired"

Unscrewing the cap,
the label's headline scrolls into view
and starts me thinking.
Should I get in line for this ride?

It's my classic dilemma
of not wanting to throw stuff away.

I don't want to overpay for dinner,
but I also like to fully enjoy dessert.

And though I've always been good at the wheel
and still have fairly quick reflexes,
it feels kinda risky,
driving without insurance
and maybe being embarrassed
running out of gas at the curb of the highway.

My kitchen attitude's more lackadaisical.
Best-eaten-before warnings
don't dull my munchies.

It doesn't bother me
if a cracker's not as crisp and crunchy.

But when Cialis's "expired" is flashing on the dash
I pause opening the car door
and wonder if the pit crew is deeply asleep
or if they're poised and ready to provide a push

when she takes the microphone in hand,
brings it to her lips,
and says,
"Gentleman, start your engines!"

¡Qué Lástima!

So we decided.

¡Está terminado!

Adding Spanish lessons
will be too much.

There's just too little time
and not enough room
in our cart.

Just yesterday
reading the *Times*
kicked church into the ditch.

And today
learning to count cards
left just a few twilight minutes
to practice sand shots,
before grilling in the dark,
and going to the open mic.

There are still more Academy nominations
screening nearby,
so dance lessons
will probably also take a hit.

Retirement's a bitch.

*¡Qué lástima!**
                              *What a pity!

In Training

I'm getting ready for the playoffs
with the rest of the retirees
who think they've mastered
the art of wasting time.

I know I'm new at this,
but they haven't a chance.

It would be a cold, cold day in August
before they could slow to my pace.

Long before starting any project,
I've learned to spend several weeks
imagining its pitfalls,
and the sun can pass from horizon to noon
while I verify a charge and write a check.

Sunday's paper lingers all week,
while last month's dust builds and gathers in each corner,
and I always measure twice-times-twice
before cutting a plank or putting a nail in drywall.

I know I have capable opponents.
I've seen them holding up traffic,
braking at shadows,
inching out of parking spaces,
and sharing long stories at the security gate.

But they've no idea how crafty I can be.

I'll touch each paper seven times,

leave my wallet at home,
lose directions,
deflate my tires,
let my tools rust,
and refuse to learn how to use my iPhone.

On competition day, I've no doubt –
they'll be finished and off to dinner
long before I'm anywhere close to done.

Guy Talk

I'm just no good at guy talk —
the latest score, current standings,
or the hottest chick.

It feels as unnatural as writing left-handed
or conversing in Turkish.

In a bucket's exchange,
I might be able to add a droplet
or a couple dribbles,
but never a stream.

My citizenship's unchallenged.
My passport's been repeatedly validated —
shaving daily,
siring a child,
throwing from my back foot,
squishing bugs and spiders,
turning my head and coughing on command.

But when locker room slang starts getting slung,
I feel like an immigrant.

Everyone else seems to have been at rehearsals,
studied their script and mastered their cues.
They know when to enter, pause, turn and talk,
while I'm still in the wings
wondering if I'm part of this scene.

Latched

I can feel it in my brow
and see it in my tight arms
locked across my chest.

The voice is sure –
sweet, welcoming and flowing
from a smiling face,
or hard and insistent,
leaning in beneath steel eyes.

But I can tell within
that I've flipped the latch,
spun the dial and closed my safe.

I'll sit and smile, listen and nod,
but I'm in retreat
and not going to engage in battle
or clink mugs and share each other's brew.

I try to stay open as long as possible,
late into the night
and deep into all sorts of babble,
and I'll welcome almost anyone in.
You don't need a tie or high heels.
You don't need a degree or thick wallet.

But sometimes the message is too bland
or laced with too much invective,
and I crank the shutters, lock the gate,
and stay inside.

Pronoun Challenged

I guess I'm just not
one of those "anybody else's" –
those "normal" people or girlfriends
who would understand.

She's smart beyond doubt,
has studied the world,
keeps up to date,
and is far more insightful than most.

But somewhere along the way,
maybe skipping grades
or spending her junior year abroad,
she became pronoun challenged.

When you know what you're talking about,
"it" is unmistakably clear.
"He" is a specific dude,
and "they" stand out from the crowd.

But without clearer clues,
I'm flying in a cloud
unable to see a runway,
while seated in the control tower
she radios to tell me
that I'm the Pilot of Idiocy.

Velcro Words

I might have to speak to Juan,
my weed control expert.

My parents were well-informed gardeners
and didn't scrimp planting my future.

I was well-coached,
got to play on the finest fields,
and they paid for quality teachers
who would often walk me through places
like where "two roads diverged in a yellow wood."

Later, I exercised alone climbing the syntax
and peering into the depths where
"man is but a walking shadow,
full of sound and fury, signifying nothing."

And when the cloud of many losses fell upon the land
I paused to slowly nourish myself
at the table of the dream
"that one day every valley shall be exalted,
every hill and mountain shall be made low,
the rough places will be made plain,
and the crooked places will be made straight."

So it wasn't surprising
when my inner critic moved to a corner lot
wrapped with windows
from which he watched my every stroke
and offered better phrasing
faster than I could move my pen.

The word, the right word, mattered,
and its capture was celebrated.

I had learned to never trust a first draft,
not to mistake rhetoric for substance,
and that a good eraser was as valuable as lead and ink.
But despite my efforts to guard my tongue,
my mouth has been stuffed with drivel.

Language mutates and can be as virulent
as the latest flu.

Hug the wrong person
and you're down with sniffles.

Watch a cutting-edge sitcom
and another strain of vapid verbiage
might infect your ear
or pitch a tent on your lips.

I've tried to protect myself,
posting "Stay Out" signs to keep them off my land
and firing public ridicule at poachers.

But some of these zombie syllables
are as inescapable as Beijing smog
and as plentiful and invasive as Asian carp.

Live long enough near these Velcro words
and they clamp onto your tongue
and erode your thinking.

I'm hoping Juan might have a secret remedy,

because you know, honestly, it's like,
well, like, they take over your mind,
and it's hard to break free,
and actually, after a while, yada yada,
you're kinda left like, whatever.

3.14.15 (9:26:53)

They were on sale
just inside the front doors.

So, when she asked,
I said, "Yes," and got the Dutch Apple.

Mathematics used to be
my favorite homework dessert.
I struggled through French,
and history put me to sleep.

But I reveled in the beauty
of the numerical mosaic –
the power of each formula,
and the facet of the universe it laid bare.

Yes, it was too much sugar for my circumference,
but this celebration's radius
wouldn't again reach my lifetime's arc,
and the top crust's interleaving matrix
was surrounded by a perfect sin-curving rim
enclosing cinnamon-flavored isosceles wedges
that I couldn't resist.

Over the next twenty-four hours
I sliced and consumed it in 3.14 parts.

NO DIVING

I know it's only three feet,
and that in every park, school and club
bold block forbidding letters would run
under the spot where I stand.

But I erase those words from my mind
and curl my toes over the rim,
drop my hands, arms and shoulders toward my feet,
and slowly tilt my hips forward,
allowing my weight to begin the fall past the edge,
then reach out, stretching toward a hidden horizon,
as I push forward from the wall.

It's just a moment's flight,
an instant's rush of air and commitment,
before I break through the splashdoor
and am surrounded by quiet.

I try to launch with the same reach
taught at the Y and lengthened in high school,
where "Ready – Set – Go's" turned the tiled silence
into a muffled echo chamber of cheers, slaps and
    breathing.

And though in just a few strokes
I'll hit a wall and need to turn,
I try to pull and glide, kick and recover,
and slice the water, just like in the open lake
on the way to the Kist Island dock
then back to the Cookie Boy bridge,
where, at ten, I arrived exhausted,

with such rubbery legs and weakened grips
that I nearly fell climbing the slick pilings,
up, above the stringers,
to stand, on the top decking,
chill, smiling and triumphant.

YOU ARE THERE

Bench Seat

for Bruce & Polly

"Up for a little nostalgia?" he asked around noon,
and returned in a '58 Olds convertible with the top down,
a broad, white leather, front bench seat,
and chrome knobs to tune the AM radio.

"Dad's car!" Then his.
Then left behind.
Then found at auction.
Washed, polished, tweaked and restored.

White sidewalls and broad, shiny hubcaps
with a red stripe like a windswept tear
bleeding from the corner of the double headlights
back along the swollen cream fender
and body-armored side door.

"Our first-date car," she said,
smiling and slipping into the back seat
while putting on her fresh summer hat
with the product tag still waving from the crown.

"Yes," he said, as his grin stretched the corner of his eyes.
"Long drives out the boulevard and along the river."

And with his left hand on the steering wheel,
his right rested quietly on the seat,
where there was no separating console.

And as I took my place in the midday glare
and we crossed over the gravel crunch to the road,

I could see the soft sunset glow
and hear The Shirelles, Bobby Rydell,
Aretha and Chubby Checker in the cool evening breeze.

Another Trim

I park with hope and fear
and, as the entry bell fades,
pull my ticket and quietly take a seat
surrounded by mirrors, barbershop babble,
and the soundtrack of a military comedy
flickering off a flat panel in the far corner.

After twenty-five years, she went south –
interstates, mountains and nights away.

Too far for a monthly visit.
Too far to continue our conversation
about children, culture and careers.

Too distant to still savor
our months of dating,
nights of laughter,
and affection that outlived love.

So now, like a bar-hopping divorcee,
I move from beer to beer,
from counter, to stool, to booth,
hoping that today's snips and razor
are in the hands of a friend.

Pam's Bagels

Shit, it's as close to home cookin'
as your sorry ass is going to get.
So quit that belly-aching and eat your food.
Who put you in charge anyhow?

This place is full of all kinds of freaks.
Every morning, someone has to get in my face.
You should be happy I'm willing to get up at four-thirty
so you can have your breakfast at seven
or whenever you decide to roll out of bed.

Yeah, it just doesn't seem to matter for most'a you guys.
You show up whenever you want –
seven, eight, nine – who cares?
Am I the only one on the clock?

And shit, you can get nearly any friggin' thing you want
    here,
and I make it all from scratch.
All of it.
So how about a smile and a thank you!
I'm tired, and I just don't have time for all that bitchin'.

Yeah, I know. I love you too.
But stay out'a my face in the mornin',
or I'm gonna deck you.

Not Pam's Bagels

Rock and roll syncopates
as the warmth of a toasted bagel
cuts the canyon chill.

Bright light on the west wall
bleaches reds to pink,
and blue-jeaned,
ball-capped,
rag-wool-sweatered Pete
pays $3 a quarter hour
to surf the net
to purchase a rifle.

Utah — land of the hardy and faithful.
Land of open spaces,
far from NYC and DC,
but within reach of anthrax fear.

Pete's friends sip coffee,
read the morning paper,
and discuss smallpox,
the weapon of choice
to maim the beautiful people.

So terror invades
the canyons of serenity —
the mesas of peace.

Mr. Artelli

I hope he got a gold watch
and dinner at the Ritz.
He was my go-to-guy
in the fourth floor Boy's Department.

A man who learned my name
and earned my mother's smile
at the end of our two-transfer streetcar ride
all the way downtown.

Before earthmovers carved a turnpike
through the Pennsylvania hills,
before interstates spider webbed the nation,
and before outer belt connectors
drove developments into pastures
and malls into asphalted fields,
he helped me find shoes that fit,
jackets that draped,
and ties that spoke of style.

Someone then invented warehouse retail,
and salespeople only knew
how to bag merchandise and work the register.

In my fourth grade class photograph,
amidst my classmates' bright smiles, folded hands,
and plaids, plains and stripes,
I alone wear a suit jacket
that falls naturally across my shoulders
with sleeves kissing my big thumb's base,
an off-white dress shirt with a flat, flared collar,

a school pin in the lapel button hole,
and a dark tie matching my hair.

I wonder if there's another photo
from a retirement island off the boot of Italy
where a fluoroscope sunset spreads a warm glow
across gray-haired men in dapper sweaters
who broadly smile as they straddle showroom stools
massaging their lover's toes.

Fence

While up my ladder
trimming the far side of the hedge,
they came around the house
looking up and down
examining the yard
and imagining a life there.

I said, "Hello"
and offered tools and help
if they decided to buy,
and in her first words
she talked about a fence.

Something to prevent her daughter
from wandering off.

It is a deep back yard
with sparse bushes and spindly trees
marking the boundaries
across which we all share views
of each other's garage doors, back patios,
and the white-pearl-on-black-velvet morning lights.

Deer pass through
seeking fresh shoots to nibble
and quiet places in the summer heat
to settle away from traffic.

After they moved in,
we rang the bell
and delivered a loaf of lemon bread

to sweeten their arrival.

And when the winter's snows had melted
and the days were no longer chill,
she emerged with her dancing, skipping daughter
and plotted where to place her garden.

But as I raked and top-dressed,
seeded and fertilized nearby,
not a word or smile was shared.

As if the fence
was already there.

Cardinal Rules

When young, I thought I had learned
all the cardinal rules.

Open the door.
Help her remove her coat.
Pull out her chair.
Walk on the curb side.
Pay the check.

Then, when I pledged a fraternity,
they taught us more.

How to receive and pass dishes.
Which silverware was for what course.
When to unfold and replace a napkin.

I even tried to learn the art of romantic verse
and delivered a few syrupy lines
in the heat of attraction.

But much later, I must have misplaced my invitation
to the next series of do's and don'ts,
and I'm still having trouble
making them second nature.

Put the toilet seat down.
Roll over when snoring.
Keep lights low and talk softly in the morning.
Never spy the scale's read-out.
Don't question memories in public.

Forgetting these new imperatives
can be costly.

The penalty box is open.

Between "Jeopardy" & "Wheel of Fortune"
for Debby & David

In the middle of the commercial break,
he popped the question.

Perhaps he was done with "Basic Math"
and had finally decided which "State Capital"
he wanted to make his own.

I had been preoccupied with "Health Care"
for more than five hundred
and "Finding My Bliss" for all the marbles.

My parents would have warned
more time on "Lucrative Careers,"
and my girlfriends might have advised
another try on "Playing the Field."

But even before Vanna crossed the stage
or Pat raised his cue cards,
I knew I wouldn't need to buy a vowel
before hitting my buzzer and saying "Yes."

Because he was a career man
who could fill in my blanks,
light my fire and quench my flame.

I had spun his wheel many times,
never landed on "Bankrupt"
and sometimes even got a "Bonus Round."

And I knew he could host my life
and would never kick me out of the game.

You are There

for Makael

Droplets smack the rain fly.
The dogs press on my feet.

In the warm, silky bag
I lay curved around the night's root.

A light breeze cools my cheek
as I blink awake to pale sunlight.

    And you are there.

I take the receipt,
slide the credit card in my wallet,
and reach my hands through the plastic loops.

The weight
stretches my neck and shoulders,
stiffens my back,
and cuts into my palms.

There's more in the cart.
The car's far across the lot.
Rain is threatening.

    And you are there.

The line is slow.
Tears fall near the casket.

It's hard to stand

so close to loss.

And you are there.

Like climbing a waterfall,
I reach from task to task
as jobs and people flood my day,

then seek shelter
in a lunchtime overhang
where I key in your number.

And you are there

The plane lifts,
arcs above the familiar,
and banks toward adventures
hiding in tomorrow's shadows.

Strange faces and food,
and maybe late night strolls
through narrow streets
where tongues croon and clack,
or high noon walks
on narrow ramparts
where the stone's been cupped
by seasons of sandal, boot, staff and horseshoe.

I reach across the armrest.

And you are there

Then, near the end of day,
as the late light brushes the sand

to a golden sheen,
while shore birds skitter
amongst the glitter at the water's edge,
and my lips mouth "beautiful"
at the altar of the bare beach
inviting us for another walk,
hand in hand,
quiet by quiet.

    You are there.
    You are there.

Moving to Safety

When the waves came over the side
Mom's grip hurt my wrist,
and there was screaming everywhere.

"Are we okay, Momma?" I asked.
"Are we okay?"

But everyone was shouting, shouting, shouting,
and I could see she didn't hear me.
Her face looked tight, her lips quivering,
and her eyes were fixed forward.

"Ahmed? Ahmed?" she called across the crowd,
and pulled me closer as we were tossed right and left,
and the water climbed my socks and my pants felt cold.

Then, like bullies on a teeter totter,
the raft tilted right and everyone slid down
where the next wave washed over us,
splashed across my hair and face,
sloshed into my open collar
and trickled down my chest and arms.

When I looked up I could see she was still seeking father,
and as she pulled me closer we dropped
and the life jacket pressed against my ears.
She was breathing hard, holding me with one hand,
moving the other back and forth,
and saying, "Sayakun bikhayr. Sayakun bikhayr."
"It'll be okay. It'll be okay."

There were others in the water,
hidden and revealed by each passing wave,
hidden and revealed by silence and shouting –
shouting and silence.

The raft disappeared. The calls got softer.
Her hand slipped off my wrist.
There were stars all across the sky.

Chuck Holes

It's the freeze-thaw-freeze cycle
that's so disappointing.

Every year we invest more and more
to construct a solid foundation and stable pavement,
as true as billiards slate
and inviting as a dance floor,
and it would be reassuring to think
this time and attention
would weather well in every season
and we could move on smoothly
in sun, rain, snow and ice.

But seemingly small storms
still create huge chuck holes
that chew my confidence.

If I mention something about her driving
the road shifts into a long, silent minefield.

And wherever I turn,
I plunge into sore spots
and slam against raw edges
that threaten an explosion
whose shock I couldn't easily absorb
and that might trigger an even more damaging
loose-lipped collision.

It makes for a long drive
when no smile breaks the clouds
and every shoulder is closed.

And it could takes weeks

of warnings, backups and detours
for the patching crew to finish their work
and get us back to easy conversation
with both "I" and "you".

Dinner Dating
for Hilary & Merle

It's not a case of pheromones
or the groin-throbbing grab of perfumed earlobes and slick
  lips
in the darkened corners of basement parties
that grow into sweaty dreams
and turn Mr. Phillips' fractions lecture into a distant echo.

No, long after the groping, affairs and honeymoons,
after diapers, camps and tuition,
interviews, transfers and titles,
packing, selling and moving,
our hunger moves from the basement to the living room.

We say hello at the doorway,
shake hands and embrace,
and follow the dance floor lead from hallway to study,
slider to deck, to house projects and art,
then sit back in the soft glow of living room light,
embracing each other's history,
fondling stories of grandchildren,
and chewing on chunks of career.

We're not looking to bed.
We're not finger-combing hair
or breathing warmth into soft kisses
at the base of each other's neck.

No, it's more a tasting of cadence and credibility.
Can we paddle in rhythm?
Do our rivers flow toward the same sea?

Are their stories seasoned with a tang
that leaves us eager for second helpings?
Is there enough laughter for dessert,
enough quiet for togetherness,
and enough sparkle for fun?

We sit, talk and share.
We offer, probe and digest.

And on the way out the door,
we measure how firm the hand,
how broad the smile and direct the eye,
and if we'd like to clear the clutter in our back seat
so we might take them home.

SEA CHESTS
OR A CARRY-ON

Christmas Then and Now
for Barbara

We used to blink alert
as if our dreams had dropped us
onto a pitch dark airfield
and all-of-a-sudden, with no warning,
a flipped switch ignited all the lights
so we could see each runway from the watchtower.

We missed it again!
Did he land?

And seeing and hearing nothing,
our urgency felt explosive,
and we'd wriggle up and out
of our winter's cocoon
and tip-toe halfway down the chill stairs,
then peek around the corner of the wall
at the unlit tree and the boxes and ribbons
now strewn beneath it.

Then, in a waterfall of excitement,
we'd tumble over each other onto the landing
and scramble to the fireplace
where the dish we'd left the night before
now held but half a cookie and none of the carrots.

And moments later, at my parents' beside,
she'd say

No!
Just your stocking.

And soon, still in our Hopalong Cassidy PJs,
we'd be at the table
struggling to peel and remove the stringy web
from the tangerines
that had been stuffed in each sock's toe,
while he would set his tripod and timer
and we'd cluster together and smile before the flash.
And she would offer us a feast
of eggs, bacon and waffles with butter and real maple
   syrup
and require us to fill our tummies
before the carnage, games and new toys.

Now it arrives wrapped
in a rare pre-dawn quiet.

No tractor lights moving across our headboard.
No rumble of heavy tires crossing the bridge.

And we linger, spooning
grateful for the freedom to ignore the clock,
and no need to race out of each other's arms.

Then seated on the couch,
we sip fresh coffee
and nibble the powdered sugar crumbles
off of her mother's favorite Sara Lee cake
amidst a modest bounty of special purchases,
but knowing that the greatest gift
is each other's hand.

And soon, across the lagoon, we see the first
of the daylong stream of squatters —

twosomes, fivesomes, and fourteensomes,
each carrying their own weapons like Normandy patrols
but wearing red wool hats and striped scarves
as they breach the hill,
amble across the flat,
and fill the fairway with laughter,
because for one day
bad shots are free.

And in the early afternoon,
if she can stand it again,
I take a good book to the couch
and lay down to read
and listen to Handel's choruses
for one last time this year.

The Thaw

It was like, like cool,
the way the kids
were all in shorts and tank tops

like even most of the boys
and wearing mostly flip flops
on the way to the rock concert

and standing in like groups
on the frat house lawns
tossing footballs, Frisbees and come-on gazes
while drinking tall plastic cups of brew

and like spring had finally popped
because, you know,
the forsythia was golden
and the crabapples were white and pink
and the light was lingering
deep into the evening

and no one seemed to care
about any homework
or upcoming examinations

just about the burst of heat
and the promise of tomorrow's summer

and we drove by slowly
and then home
remembering our college days

before we gave up smoking
when we, like, took cancer seriously.

Eating Alone

Two kingfishers are arguing over territory.
They are flying close above the water
pockmarked by a fine morning mist.

And as they swoop and dive, avoid and attack,
they are firing volleys of chatter
that sound like bursts of small caliber machine guns,
but we know they are saying,

"Get away from my breakfast.
There's another cafeteria beyond the bridge."

The beach was bare tonight,

like an emptied bone white platter
abandoned on the sideboard,
as doors shut,
lights turn on,
and guests aim their cars homeward.

A few gulls
picked at the crumbs
left behind,

and a crust of moonlight
sopped up the juices
lingering by the rim.

Without Ink

I was raised a different way
in another era.

My notebook margins were cramped
with snakes, ropes and chains,
coiled and twisting,
fanged, knotted and linked,
and with daggers in bright light
or stabbed into hearts and dripping blood.

Eagles were too hard to draw,
but an occasional crude talon
gripped my pencil and held the name
of my last dance partner.

We dribbled in sleeveless jerseys,
swam in skimpy Speedos
and were taught to admire
David's relaxed power and thin waist
and Venus's unblemished beauty,
although she lost her arms.

Some World War survivors wept their history
and rolled their sleeves to show
the numbers above their wrists.
But those marks merely whispered.
Their indelible pain flowed in their tears,
cracked voice and labored breath.

The rest of us showed our loyalties
with a lapel pin or necklace,

a sweatshirt, letter jacket, or held hand.

It would be wrong to think us fickle.
We kissed with passion and pledged our allegiances
with straight backs, clear eyes and steady hands.

But in the end we were free
to experiment with our signature,
reconsider our mates and faith,
explore other schools of art
and move on without erasure or surgery.

Rainy Days

When days of sun turn into rain
and clouds sit still upon the land,
we huddle inside as if in pain.

The water puddles near each drain
and drums the roof, a one-man band,
while washing gutters of every stain,

and as if in a station we await the train
to stop so we can take the hand
of a skillful author who's worked to gain

our full imagination and can claim
to hold our interest with a plan
to walk us through a plot that's plain

but has some unexpected strains
of ironic twists and schemes so grand
that the hours fall as if they're slain

till darkness curtains off the land
and though we still hear the waves of rain,
we take a glass of wine in hand
and drink to a day unexpectedly grand.

Mouse Bedding

Restoring order, I clean the attic,
discarding tax files, college notes, expired warranties,
making room for current files.

Towers of unlabeled boxes
sit heavy in the aisle –
relics of rewiring projects,
needing to be restacked
near the eaves.

Freed up space from Goodwill donations
is filled with summer clothes
in plastic bags.

Summer fans, discarded lamps,
and Aunt Maude's table
are nestled between or balanced on
the piles of stuff we save
to share with grandkids,
furnish another home,
or keep our hearts from aching
as we say goodbye
to our treasured past.

Old sheets are spread
to ward off dust.

Away from the heat of the two bare bulbs
suspended from the center beam
the coming winter chills my hands.

More room downstairs.
More order above.
Good mouse bedding
for the darkest days ahead.

Late Night Interruptions

Each night lately, I lie awake
and try to tune in sleep.

I switch the channels
from side to back,
from pillows to none.

But my thoughts
remain as bright and active as Times Square
where my To-Do List scrolls
in big, bold letters.

I tug the blankets around my shoulders
and try to snuggle into the lullaby
of deep breathing and a flight to the shore
where the sunlight sparkles on the rhythmic surf
and I can quietly stroll along the pristine sand.

But three strides into my walk
emergency notices are again flashing on the screen
and a network news anchor interrupts
the previously scheduled program
with the most recent update on the breaking story
of not-to-be-forgotten chores.

We've lived in this house twenty years,
with a clear signal and rich dreams
without commercial interruptions
or annoying static.

And now that we're shedding stuff

and moving to a whole new neighborhood,
I'm hoping that once we're settled
our sound and stable, late night service
will be restored.

Sea Chests or a Carry-On

I'm trying to pack
for the rest of my life,
and I'm having trouble quieting the debate:
will I be happier
with sea chests or a carry-on?

We've made firm reservations
for a smaller place.
We're past the refund point,
and I'd like to feel relaxed
believing it will turn out fine.

But it's still hard
moving my appetite
from the cargo bay
to the overhead bin.

As I struggle to sort our stuff
and split the stream
between take, donate, sell or discard,
I'm trying to remember life's lessons
to help me untie my fears
and lessen our load.

Returning from China,
we had enough pills, creams and wipes
to stock a small pharmacy.

After each canoe trip
there were always uneaten snacks,
unopened soup mixes,

and plump peanut butter tubes
we had portaged through the bush
and hung from a high limb beyond a bear's reach,
only to bring back home
to reshelve or trash.

And today, my closet remains stuffed
with enough suits and ties
to attire all offensive and defensive starters
for their ride to the next game,
even though I no longer set a morning alarm,
and if I remain in bed well after dawn,
no office calls to discover why
I haven't arrived.

The glue is long lasting,
and change is slow.

I love the weightless feeling
each time I leave
more boxes of books
on the university loading dock.

Then, when I discover voids
in the local library's stacks
and lending database,
my chest feels heavy again.

If the title on its spine
doesn't haunt me from a shelf,
will I even remember
I still want to read it?

There's lots to be said
for the simple life.

You only need one spoon to eat soup,
a few peas have more flavor,
and a wall with one painting
allows it to sing more fully.

I've dabbled in Thoreau country
but can't say I've assimilated
all its customs.

I wish there were a Prius engineer
who could quickly and easily redesign
my holding habits,
so I might travel more efficiently
with less highway noise in my head.

Getting Back in Shape

After twenty years together
our attic looked in the mirror.

Having heard us talk about selling
she decided she'd gotten fat.

Just like most Americans
she'd consumed too much fast food –
an empty corner here,
a couple of boxes there,
and always room for dessert,
especially do-it-later parfaits.

"No one will love me like this,"
she moaned,
then shoved two fingers down her throat
and vomited storage bins and boxes
down the stairs and all throughout the house.

Tax records and death certificates,
college notes and children's toys,
golf clubs and camping supplies,
recipes, LPs, cassette and video tapes,
computer cables, clothing and china.

And with each retch
she coughed up spiders and mites,
dust and decay that blanketed our rugs
and left a sticky film on our fingers.

And even after weeks of work,

when her trainer stopped by,
she still had more to do to get trim.

But that's what everyone wants these days —
a neurotically perfectionistic, anorexic attic,
no personality and a virgin's demeanor.

Like she's never been touched
and is just waiting to be invited on a date,
where she can gorge herself,
till she's full.

Still in the Room

And there he was,
ashes scattered in the rose garden,
but still in the room.

Remodeling challenged,
we moved ahead at an anxious crawl,
preparing the way for new shelves,
but fearful of irreversible mistakes.

Ripping old braces from the wall
revealed its fragility
as the wonder bar broke its surface
and left a gaping hole.

What should we do?
How best to support the anticipated weight
of dresses, coats, slacks, and costumes?

But Dad's sure carpentry still remained,
sketched on the remaining wall
and securely anchored in place.

Reminders to find the hidden studs,
nail braces to them,
and position the rest between.

Gone, but still guiding.
Silent, but still talking.
Absent, but still leading.
Pointing us toward a better path.

Ties

Years before church or prom, interviews and position,
standing by my father, looking in the mirror,
smiling and laughing as he guided the silk
twice around and up, then back down through.

Standing by my father looking in the mirror,
where later we'd be with a razor and cream –
twice around and up, then back down through.
Another shared saying from father to son.

Like the razor and cream so many years later
as gently I pulled across the skin on his cheek,
reciting more sayings from father and back,
his lessons in my hands as the light moved away.

And I still pull gently, stretch the skin on my cheek,
match a belt to my pants, and a tie to a jacket.
Twice around and up, then back down through,
standing by my father, looking in the mirror.

Dribble, Drive & Shoot

Like an eager lover
the ball returns to your hand,
where you can caress it with your fingertips
and lavish in its familiar curvature,
like the swell of a crystal goblet
while swirling a fine Bordeaux.

And the ball's quick kiss
comes through your wrist and forearm
that welcome it like Aunt Grace's embrace
after she passes the security gate
and throws her arms wide
as she runs to you
after her European summer.

Then the ball's dissipating climb
spring loads the travel agent in your bicep
that's been monitoring all the best deals,
and in the next instant it issues a ticket
to a flight across court,
a cruise toward the rim,
or a quick drive through the canyon of bigs.

Like a Michener opus,
it's a game of generations.

From the wobbly, plastic hoop
that shattered the gold glass globe
dangling near the bottom Christmas tree branch,
to the lowered elementary school baskets
that begged for a quick toss

on our way back to class
when kickball hadn't fully exhausted us,

and to the summer camp's uneven, dusty, dirt court,
where the ball would carom off roots and stones
and we'd dash into the nearby brush,
not stopping to survey for poison oak or brambles,
before the ball reached the drop-off to the lake.

Then came the dark brown, plywood backboard
we'd painted to match the outdoor trim —
soon followed by an afternoon
installing Plexiglas garage windows.

The rough weekend jazz
of our shoes scuffing the driveway
was eventually replaced by a soprano chorus
of rubber-on-varnish squeaks
echoing off the field house rafters
during practices where Coach
would shoot a pass to your head
if you took your eye off the ball.

Then toting handed down, home washed uniforms,
we took quiet bus rides to cold, cramped locker rooms
and ranks of shouting faces, one yard from the sideline,
where we sometimes jumped and laughed at the buzzer
but often retreated to a shower
and a longer ride home.

Today, remote in hand, I sit on the couch
eating my daily Caramel Pretzel Klondike,
or on a rare night out, empty-handed,
after our waitress has just warned me to be careful

because the plate with my favorite spaghetti pie
is oven hot,
I just monitor the screen
on the far wall beyond the booth.

And as I watch and overhear the commentary
I both see and feel the game.

My body leans into a drive.
My shoulders square to the basket,
and I feel the tiniest spring in my toes,
as if I were on the court and rising up
with the ball above my head,
where it's nestled like a dove in my palm
just before I let it fly
in a smooth, rim-bound arc
with even backspin
and dreams of another score.

The Harrow

When I tug it from the clamp
snugging it to the garage wall
my hand reaches into the past.

To the backyard garden
where my grandfather stands
his hands poised at the top of the shaft,
as his weeding and tilling were interrupted
for the one, grainy, five-by-seven
that sits on my dresser
and greets me every morning.

He looks over his shoulder,
squinting in the sunlight baking his back,
and still wearing the long sleeves, vest and tie
from his day at work.

There was nothing permanent-pressed
about his world.

It was an age of migration and planting,
a time of sturdy fibers
that slowly cupped to your knees and elbows,
frayed at the collar,
and swung from a line
stretched from the back door.

A time when green-visored engineers
hunched over drawing boards
as they pulled lead along t-squares and triangles.

When rough hands would anchor a length of ash
to be turned and rounded,
and wood flakes would cluster in forearm hairs
as a drawknife was slowly pulled across its surface.

And when a craftsman's eye
would shape the shaft's narrow neck
to lead my grandfather's, my father's and my hand
to the harrow's sweet balance point,
where we could comfortably cradle and caress it
in the crook of our fingers
on our way to drawing its tines
through the rich earth
as we dreamt of a better life.

Winter Hunting

Our roads don't ice.
Our trees don't glitter.

We've sold our shovels
and would need an overnight
to find a flake or drift.

But winter wraps wool around us still
and tries to push us indoors
with rain and wind and chill.

And as the daytime doorway tightens,
we burrow like moles
through tree-blackened, starless tunnels
clearing our eyes with high-beam blinks
as we wind our way out or back home.

In these dark, dark days we thirst for light,
for bright blue mornings
turning frost to steam,
for cloudless afternoons
spreading nap-time heat across a couch,
and for the sundown glow
of auditorium arias and jazz club scat.

Doorway bells ring "give".
Snowy melodies prance "buy".
And our mailboxes spew
cataracts of colorful catalogues
that try to lure us with new and better.

But our closets are full.
We've had our fill of stuff.
And we're hunting for more elusive game.

For gifts that will feed us past spring.

For nuggets of everyday love
dipped in chocolate swirls.

For old friendships wrapped in new stories,
and new friendships
sprinkled with honesty, laughter and promise.

For art still warm from the oven.

And for a few well-ironed adventures
that aren't too broad in the shoulders
or too deep in the pocket
and that feel comfortable and exciting to the touch.

Winter Rituals

Christmas arrives like a high tide
carrying good will ashore
and scattering presents across the living room floor

where they wait
for the New Year's Eve beach patrol
bent on restoring order

and clearing the way
for a champagne toast
and hours of bowl games

after the sun sets
and fireworks climb and spread
across the night sky.

WAITING FOR
AN OPEN DOOR

Writing Tools

Stolen pens write best,
like those lifted from a maid's cart
or not returned to a desk clerk.

They feel alive, ready for risk,
unafraid to shit on the page.

They travel in my passenger seat,
refuse to wear seat belts,
dare me to ignore stop signs

encourage racing from impulse to ink,
no thought for crossing traffic
or innocents in church or school zones.

My mother used to preach,
"Bad tasting medicines are better,"

as if disgust has the power
to unclog the arteries of a full life.

I'm doing my part.
If needed, please send bail.

Waiting for an Open Door

I was too early to get inside.

Lights were on,
and a few cars were in the lot,
but the door was closed.

Still, I was lucky.

The Island Beautification Association had funded
two long benches with sturdy metal arms,
glossy varnished wooden slats,
and a commemorative brass plaque
screwed into the center of the second top railing.

So, under cover of the grand portico,
listening to the morning birds
and traffic on the nearby highway,
brushing mosquitos from my forearms,
and watching a young chameleon
exploring the pavement near my feet,
I could sit and search for something to write.

I never know when the door will open
or if there will be a bench to support my first words
and allow them to rest and dwell,
breathe and amble in a new day's quiet possibilities.

The outside world is more predictable.
Someone's made a schedule.
Others need their pay.

My muse keeps her own hours,
takes vacations as she wishes,
and often travels furniture-free
or with stuff that's still en route.

Workout Time

I need to head to the gym.
My notebook's been closed for weeks,
and I haven't lifted a single line
above my waist.

Thinking doesn't do it.

I need to get my pen on a treadmill
and keep it moving till sweat blots a page.

At this rate, I'll lose my strength and flexibility
and be unable to type my way
out of an unfinished thought
when all that's needed is a dash of risk
and a curl of reflection.

Not Only Martine

After I helped move the furniture,
rolled the carpet and re-combed my hair,
Maman took me aside.

She likely didn't know how often or how far
Martine's hand crept up my thigh
during our long family lunches,
but she guessed
whose dark Moroccan eyes I hoped to see
and whose waist I dreamed of pulling near.

So away from everyone else,
in the kitchen hallway,
Maman brought me close
looked up and whispered,

*Tu danseras avec tous
les jeunes filles!*

You will dance with all
the girls!

She meant to teach the gentleman's way,
but in her hushed, insistent voice
she also shared the secret
to opening the door of life and art,
because we're all really
on a series of blind dates.

Each day arrives in a different skirt.
Only a fool tries to smell yesterday's perfume

or kiss tomorrow's lips.

And even when I've straightened the clutter,
set the table with clean white pages,
plenty of crisp chilled ink is standing by,
and I'm waiting for the doorbell to ring,
I've learned Maman was right.

I might be yearning for a dark-eyed inspiration
in stiletto heels and a low cut blouse
to slip inside, moisten her lips, and unzip my pen.

But whatever image steps out of the shadows,
she's the one with whom I must dance.

I might not yet have heard the band,
felt its rhythm or recognized its melody,
but that is the moment to take her hand,
walk to the floor and bring her into my arms
because she is ready and has risked being seen.

And since smiles come wrapped with many ribbons,
until we dance, I will never know
if this will be a casual acquaintance,
a short affair or lifelong love,

if the dance will be dull
or full of laughter,

if the band will take a break
or play on and on,

if she'll tiptoe away during the night
or share breakfast at dawn.

And all the while,
I have the feeling
others are hanging back,
watching our moves,
deciding whether I'd be a worthy partner
when she's done.

Uncorking a Poem

After peeling the title
and tugging the first few lines,
swirl, sniff and sip it like wine,
then sink in your teeth
and chew it like jerky.

Lay in it. Roll in it.
Get its scent deep in your fur.

Pull it over your shoulders.
Slip your arms up its sleeves,
and see how it fits
and if it goes with your outfit,
your mood, your smiles, or your tears.

Rake it across your past
and watch where it clings
and slides into crevices.

Let it bake in the oven
till crisp and caramelized
then taste and decide
if you'd like to serve it to friends.

Follow it's flashlight into the forest
while it probes the darkness.
See if it uncovers any hidden treasures.

Hold its hand by the shore
as you breathe the salt air

and listen to the surf's song.
Then kiss and say goodbye.

Going to the Dump

It's not really "the dump" —
more a way-station between us
and some mountain of trash
far from view, where birds flock
and no one wants to be downwind.

Most hire a service and only take the short walk
from the kitchen basket
to the trash can near the garage,
then wave twice weekly
as bags are carried down the driveway
to the truck's open jaws.

But the rest of us want more —
money in our wallet,
the taste of self-righteousness
as we sort and deposit recyclables,
and membership in the dance
to keep our world safe, clean and beautiful.

Driving away, my car feels spacious
with lots of room for new indulgences,
space for the next empty bottle,
can of soup, unread newspaper,
orange rind, apple core, love letter.

My Missing Muse

My muse went on vacation.
I get depressed when she's not home.
I launched a search across the nation.
I try to cope but feel alone.

I get depressed when she's not home.
When she left the fridge was bare.
I try to cope but feel alone.
I can't cook without her there.

When she left the fridge was bare.
Nothing to nibble. Nothing to try.
I can't cook without her there.
She didn't even kiss me goodbye.

Nothing to nibble. Nothing to try.
I miss her singing and her joy.
She didn't even kiss me goodbye.
I wish she wasn't being so coy.

I miss her singing and her joy.
She was my lover all last year.
I wish she wasn't being so coy.
Her absence leaves me full of fear.

She was my lover all last year.
She cooked. She cleaned. She polished.
Her absence leaves me full of fear.
I'm starving and feeling demolished.

She cooked. She cleaned. She polished.
My muse went on vacation.
I'm starving and feeling demolished.
I need her back for recreation.
She'd better have a good explanation.

"Let a dog run across your poem."
(from Billy Collins)

And then he advised,
let a dog run across your poem.

It could be the wet dog
he wrote about,

the one everyone shunned
as he roamed around the bar
and they ate and drank.

Or it could be one of the tiny poodles
with fluffed fur and a pink ribbon
that my wife hopes
will keep her company
in the front seat
as we drive across America
and stop by each tree
of every rest stop.

Or it could be that broad-shouldered
square-browed retriever,
the dog of my youth and dreams,
who could have been
the Marlboro Man's companion
and who'd love to snuggle close
in a wilderness tent
warming each frosty night.

But before I let any dog
tramp his dirty paws

across my clean pages,
it might be wise to decide
how often and for how long
we might want to return to Paris,
explore South America,
and cruise to St. Petersburg.

Mockingbird DJ

Rain was everywhere –
in the pockmarked stream,
bouncing palms,
slick deck shine,
and splatter on each pane.

Wind whipped down the channel
and moaned around each pillar.

But thrown about high in the tree,
he still held his post
and sang about the light
hidden behind the thick overcoat clouds.

Like a wild and wanton disk jockey,
he played the top forty
and offered free tickets to every listener
looking for the first days of spring.

About the Author

Bill Newby was born and raised in Cleveland, Ohio where he worked as an English teacher, school administrator, college advisor and adjunct lecturer. He and his wife, Barbara Hill-Newby, currently reside on South Carolina's Hilton Head Island.

He considers himself an "everyday writer" – using poetry and fiction to record and explore moments of celebration, complaint, concern and comedy.

His work has appeared in *Bluffton Breeze, Ohio Teachers Write, Palm Beach Poetry Festival Fish Tales Contest, Panoplyzine, Sixfold, Whiskey Island,* and the Island Writers' Network's *Time and Tide* and *Ebb and Flow.*

He can be reached at: Bill.Newby.wordsmith@gmail.com